THE MAGNIFICENT BOOK OF ROCKS AND MINERALS

THE MAGNIFICENT BOOK OF ROCKS AND MINERALS

ILLUSTRATED BY
Isabel Aracama and Simon Mendez

WRITTEN BY
John Farndon

weldon**owen**

Written by John Farndon
Illustrated by Isabel Aracama and Simon Mendez
Consultant: Dr. Freya George

weldonowen
Copyright © Weldon Owen Children's Books, 2025

All rights reserved. No part of this publication may be reproduced, distributed, or transmitted in any form or by any means, including photocopying, recording, or other electronic or mechanical methods, without the prior written permission of the publisher, except in the case of brief quotations embodied in critical reviews and certain other noncommercial uses permitted by copyright law.

Published by Weldon Owen Children's Books
An imprint of Weldon Owen International, L.P.
A subsidiary of Insight International, L.P.
PO Box 3088
San Rafael, CA 94912
www.insighteditions.com

Weldon Owen Children's Books
Designer: Clive Savage
Editors: George Maudsley and Eliza Kirby
Managing Editor: Mary Beth Garhart

Insight Editions
CEO: Raoul Goff
Senior Production Manager: Greg Steffen

ISBN: 979-8-88674-051-6

Manufactured in China by Insight Editions
First printing, March 2025. RRD0325
10 9 8 7 6 5 4 3 2 1

Insight Editions, in association with Roots of Peace, will plant two trees for each tree used in the manufacturing of this book.

MIX
Paper | Supporting responsible forestry
FSC® C144853

Introduction

Our planet is made of rocks and minerals—they are the building blocks of the Earth. Deep underground, some rocks are so hot that they exist in a liquid form called magma. As magma reaches the surface, it cools to create Earth's rocky crust. Rocks are the source of nearly all the materials we use to make things, from stones for building to the metals in machinery. The oldest rocks are more than four billion years old and have survived everything the planet can throw at them. Rocks are being worn down and recycled all the time before being remade in the furnace of Earth's interior.

Minerals are natural solids that form crystals. Nearly all mineral crystals are tiny and dull, but occasionally they grow big, hard, and shiny. These are what give us gemstones. There are about 5,800 kinds of mineral, and one way of distinguishing them is by their hardness. This can be measured on a scale increasing from 1 to 10 called the Mohs scale. When a mix of these minerals occurs together naturally, we call them rocks.

The Magnificent Book of Rocks and Minerals is a celebration of the rocks and minerals that make up Earth's surface. Read about super-tough granite rock, brought up molten hot from the Earth's interior to form towering mountains. Marvel at fluorite, which glows different colors under different lights, and find out why sparkling gems such as ruby and emerald are so precious. Discover lapis lazuli, used in the death mask of the ancient Egyptian boy king Tutankhamun, and see how moonstone seems to trap light within it. Learn how rocks and minerals are made, which are the rarest, and why some minerals are not minerals at all.

Embark on a journey of discovery as you explore some of our planet's most stunning natural creations.

Fact file

Substance: Mineral

Type: Silicate

Found: Pegmatites, hydrothermal veins

Hot spots: Brazil, Tanzania, Mozambique, Nigeria, Madagascar, Pakistan

Typical colors: Pale blue to light green

Properties: 7.5–8 hardness

Contents

Fluorite	8	Coal	26
Agate	10	Aquamarine	28
Emerald	12	Sandstone	30
Lapis lazuli	14	Jade	32
Opal	16	Galena	34
Sulfur	18	Marble	36
Gneiss	20	Hematite	38
Ruby	22	Unakite	40
Moonstone	24	Gold	42

Turquoise	44	Cinnabar	62
Gypsum	46	Peridotite	64
Basalt	48	Limestone	66
Amber	50	Diamond	68
Calcite	52	Tourmaline	70
Granite	54	Obsidian	72
Topaz	56	Amethyst	74
Copper	58	Malachite	76
Halite	60	Garnet	78

Fluorite

Calcium fluoride

- Fluorite forms large, colorful crystals but is rarely used as a gem because it is so soft. This means it is too fragile for jewelry.

- Pure fluorite is colorless, but traces of other minerals in it mean it is found in a wide range of colors. For example, the presence of yttrium makes these fluorite stones lavender colored. Even the same fluorite crystal can sometimes be more than one color.

- Heat and radiation can change fluorite's color. In fact, fluorite crystals start to glow when they are heated. If exposed to the Sun for long, a crystal's color may fade away altogether.

- Most kinds of fluorite glow blue under ultraviolet light. This gives us the word *fluorescent*. The ultraviolet light reacts with ingredients in the mineral to make the crystal shine.

Fact file

Substance: Mineral

Type: Salt

Found: Veins in pegmatite and limestone

Hot spots: Alps; Harz, Germany; Tennessee, USA; China

Typical colors: Many

Properties: 4 hardness

Fluorite's glow under ultraviolet light depends on how the impurities slightly alter the crystal. Different kinds of light can make fluorite glow different colors.

 This mineral can be used to create hydrofluoric acid for making fluoride. This is a substance added to toothpaste and water to keep people's teeth strong.

 Blue John is a famous purple-blue variety of fluorite. It is mined in England and used for luxury household ornaments, such as bowls, jewelry, or goblets.

Agate

Silicon dioxide

- Agate is a type of chalcedony, a special kind of quartz. Chalcedonies look like stones rather than crystals because the crystals are too tiny to see. When they are polished, they become shiny, shimmering gemstones.

- This mineral begins its life as a hole in solid rock. Over time, water filled with dissolved minerals oozes into this space. As the space dries out, layers of minerals are left behind on the inside of the hole. These different-colored layers are what make agate stripy.

- Agate with white bands alternating with stripes of black, brown, or red are called onyx. Green agate is known as moss agate.

- Most agates sold in stores are colored by people to make them look more attractive.

- Agate is one of the birthstones for May. Some people believe the stone to be soothing and to bring peace of mind.

Fact file

Substance: Mineraloid
Type: Quartz
Found: Holes in volcanic rocks
Hot spots: Brazil, Uruguay
Typical colors: Varied, stripy
Properties: 6.5–7 hardness

Chalcedonies other than agate include jasper, carnelian, and chrysoprase. The Romans carved pictures into jasper stones to make rings and pendants. Ancient warriors wore carnelian pendants because they thought its blood-red color would give them courage.

Emerald

Beryllium aluminum silicate

- Emerald is one of the four "precious gems," along with diamond, ruby, and sapphire. It is cherished for its vivid green color.

- Like diamonds, emeralds can be millions of years old. They formed from hot fluids in metamorphic rocks or volcanic pipes. Because they were made deep down in Earth's crust, emeralds can usually only be reached by mining.

- This mineral is a kind of beryl. The presence of chromium and vanadium is what makes it green.

- Emeralds are very tough and can exist on their own long after the rock they were embedded in has broken down. This means they can sometimes be found where they have been washed into streams.

Fact file

Substance: Mineral
Type: Silicate
Found: Metamorphic rocks, pegmatites
Hot spots: Colombia, Brazil
Typical color: Green
Properties: 7.5–8 hardness

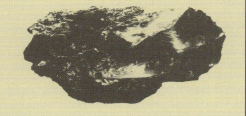

The world's biggest emerald is the Bahia emerald, weighing 750 pounds (340 kilograms). It was dug up in Bahia, Brazil, in 2001 and stored for a time in New Orleans, where it was almost lost when the warehouse was left flooded for weeks after Hurricane Katrina. Now it is kept safely in Los Angeles.

 In 1622, the Spanish ship *Nuestra Señora de Atocha* left Cuba carrying 71 pounds (32 kilograms) of emeralds from the famous Muzo mine in Colombia. The ship sank two days out of port, but its wreck was found in 1985 with up to half a billion dollars of treasure on board.

Lapis lazuli

Metamorphic rock

- Lapis lazuli is a vivid gemstone made mainly from a blue mineral called lazurite. The deep blue comes from the sulfur in lazurite. Sulfur is normally yellow, but its combination with other chemicals in lazurite turns it blue.

- This rock often contains small amounts of yellow pyrite and white calcite alongside sulfur. When they catch the light, the spots of pyrite and calcite in the blue of lapis lazuli can look like stars in a night sky.

- Lapis stones form in veins and as masses in marble. Veins are bands of minerals that run through a rock like raspberry in ripple ice cream. They form when hot, salty water moves through rocks.

- These stones are very rare. In ancient times, they were mined only in Afghanistan. They have since also been discovered near Lake Baikal in Siberia, Russia, and in the Andes Mountains in Chile.

- Lapis lazuli, like another blue gem—sapphire—is a birthstone for September.

Fact file

Substance: Rock

Type: Silicate, sulfate, and carbonate

Found: Veins in marble

Hot spots: Afghanistan, Russia, Chile

Typical color: Blue

Properties: 5–6 hardness

Lapis lazuli was much treasured in the ancient world. The ancient Egyptians carved lapis into scarab beetle amulets to keep evil away. They also used it on the famous gold funeral mask of the Egyptian boy king Tutankhamun.

 The vivid blue paint ultramarine was made from crushed lapis. Art buyers in the Italian Renaissance, about 500 years ago, paid extra for paintings using ultramarine. This is why artists often used the color on important figures, such as the Virgin Mary. It let buyers show off their wealth and religious devotion.

Opal

Silicone dioxide with water

- ⬢ Unlike most other gems, opals are not crystals. They are mineraloids—solid natural substances that do not have the crystals of a true mineral. Opals are more like blobs of hard jelly and contain a lot of water.

- ⬢ Opals are made from silica and water. This mixture is found in nearly all rocks and can seep into different surfaces. It is why opals can form in cracks in almost any rock and can also be found in fossils or ancient bits of wood.

- ⬢ Common opals are shiny black or milky white, but precious opal is filled with shimmering rainbow colors. The shimmer is called opalescence. Common or "potch" opal is used for sandpaper and is not a gemstone.

- ⬢ NASA's Curiosity rover has discovered opal on the surface of Mars. Water is needed for opal to form, so this tells us that Mars may once have been much wetter and potentially hospitable to life.

Fact file

Substance: Mineraloid

Type: Silicate

Found: Globules in rocks and fossils

Hot spots: Australia, Ethiopia, USA, Mexico

Typical colors: Black, white, rainbow

Properties: 5.5–6 hardness

Fire opals are orange opals found especially in Mexico. They get their color from traces of iron oxide. Fire opals can also be black. These are found in the Virgin Valley in Nevada, USA.

Sulfur

Native sulfur

- Sulfur is both a chemical element and a mineral. An element is a substance that cannot be broken down further. Elements found in the ground are called native elements. Sulfur is the only native element besides diamond that is not a metal.

- Sulfur is mostly found as a powdery stone or crust and sometimes as crystals like these ones. It is often seen in crusts around hot springs and smoking volcanic chimneys called fumaroles. But whatever form it is in, it is nearly always very yellow.

- This element is known for being very stinky. It gives off a smell of rotten eggs, and its gas can be poisonous.

- In the past, sulfur was known as brimstone because it burns. Brimstone means burning stone. The word is associated with God's punishment in some religions.

- Sulfur can form when bacteria alter minerals in underground gypsum deposits. These deposits typically provide sulfur for us to use.

Fact file

Substance: Mineral
Type: Native element
Found: Hot springs, volcanic chimneys
Hot spots: China, Canada, Russia, USA
Typical color: Yellow
Properties: 1.5–2.5 hardness

Sulfur has many uses. In the past, it was often included in gunpowder. Its most important use today is for making sulfuric acid. This is needed for making fertilizers for growing crops, as well as car batteries, detergents, and rubber tires.

 When fossil fuels such as oil and coal are burned, they release sulfur chemicals into the atmosphere. The chemicals can combine with water in the air to make sulfuric acid. This can fall as acid rain, which can do terrible damage to forests and soil.

Gneiss

Metamorphic rock

- Gneiss is a metamorphic rock. Metamorphic rocks are formed when rocks are altered deep underground due to the Earth's scorching heat or intense pressure.

- The word metamorphic is from the ancient Greek words for "change form." This indicates how heat and pressure change the way minerals in the rock bind together, turning the rock from one type to another.

- This rock usually forms deep down in the Earth, where heat and pressure are exceptionally intense—especially beneath mountains thrown up by the crunching together of parts of Earth's surface.

- Gneiss is the toughest rock of all. This is why some of the world's oldest rocks are gneisses. A vast area of gneiss in northwest Canada is up to four billion years old. It is one of the oldest surviving bits of Earth's crust.

Fact file

Substance: Rock

Type: Metamorphic

Found: Mountain roots

Hot spots: Canada, USA, India, Scandinavia

Typical colors: Stripy, black, and gray

Properties: Coarse grains

- During metamorphism, gneiss's dark and light minerals are smeared into alternating stripes, like a candy cane. Dark bands contain more magnesium- and iron-based minerals, and lighter bands have more feldspar or quartz.

- Different kinds of gneiss are created depending on which rock was squeezed to make them. Some rocks, such as basalt, are changed into "garnet gneiss," which is rich in the mineral garnet. It may even contain precious garnet gemstones.

Ruby

Aluminum oxide

- Ruby is a rare, superhard mineral made of a type of corundum, one of the hardest substances on Earth. Rubies formed in metamorphic rocks such as marble long ago. Corundum's toughness means some have survived for more than three billion years.

- The strength of corundum, which makes ruby hard, means it is useful in making a powder used for sharpening knives. Another variety of corundum is sapphire.

- The best rubies were once found in rivers in Myanmar, where they were washed after the rocks they were formed in were worn away over time. Recently, many have been mined in Aappaluttoq in Greenland.

- In 1960, Theodore Maiman produced the first ever laser beam when he bounced light through a human-made ruby.

Fact file

Substance: Mineral
Type: Oxide
Found: Metamorphic rocks
Hot spots: Greenland, Myanmar
Typical color: Deep red
Properties: 9 hardness

The Black Prince's ruby sits in the Imperial State Crown, first worn by Queen Victoria of England and now worn by British monarchs during their coronations. However, it is not a ruby at all. It is actually a dark red spinel, a different kind of gemstone.

 A ruby called the Sunrise Ruby once sold for a staggering $30 million. It possesses the desirable deep-red color known as "pigeon's blood" that Myanmar rubies are famous for.

Moonstone

Potassium aluminum silicate

- Moonstone gets its name from the way it seems to glow from within with a softly shimmering milky-blue light. As the stone is turned, the glow appears to move with it, like moonlight floating on water.

- The glow within moonstone is called adularescence or schiller. The word comes from a famous site for finding moonstones at Mount Adular in Switzerland.

- The ancient Romans were amazed by the light in moonstone and associated it with Diana, their goddess of the Moon.

- This mineral was made famous in the artistic period known as Art Nouveau by jewelers such as René Lalique and Louis Comfort Tiffany.

Fact file

Substance: Mineral
Type: Silicate
Found: Metamorphic rocks
Hot spots: Alps, Armenia, Myanmar, Sri Lanka
Typical colors: Blue-white, rainbow
Properties: 6–6.5 hardness

Moonstone belongs to a huge range of minerals called feldspars. These are found in just about every rock because they form from magma. Feldspars are divided into two big groups—plagioclase feldspars and potassium-rich feldspars such as moonstone.

 Moonstone forms when two types of feldspar minerals—orthoclase feldspar and albite—are mixed under extreme pressures and high temperatures. As the new mineral cools down, it splits into the layers that create its shimmering effect.

25

Coal

Organic rock

- Coal is the only rock that burns. It was the main fuel for industry for nearly 200 years, used to power steam engines, produce heat to make steel, and generate electricity.

- Coal is a fossil fuel. It is made from the rotten and crushed remains of plants that lived long ago. They were gradually buried deeper, squeezed, fossilized, and turned into seams—layers of hard carbon.

- This rock is mostly made from carbon as well as small amounts of hydrogen, sulfur, oxygen, and nitrogen.

- Much of our coal came from swamp plants that lived some 300 million years ago, in a time called the Carboniferous period.

- Most good-quality coal has to be dug from the ground in deep mines. The hardest, blackest, most pure-burning coal is found very deep down and is known as anthracite.

Fact file

Substance: Rock

Type: Sedimentary

Found: Mostly in seams underground

Hot spots: USA, Russia, Australia, China

Typical color: Black

Properties: Fine grains

Burning coal puts a lot of dirty soot into the air. It also releases carbon dioxide, a greenhouse gas that upsets Earth's climate. For this reason, the burning of coal is being phased out.

Aquamarine

Beryllium aluminum silicon oxide

- This pale blue mineral is a type of beryl called aquamarine. Different amounts of chemicals give beryl different colors. Iron makes blue aquamarine, a little less iron makes yellow heliodor, and manganese makes pink morganite.

- This type of beryl usually forms in coarse, mineral-rich bands called pegmatites in granite rocks. It is also found in veins and gaps in the rock where it has been altered by hot volcanic liquids.

- Aquamarine is one of the birthstones for March. Its name comes from the Latin word for seawater because of its sealike color. *Aqua* means water and *marina* means "of the sea" in Latin.

- The mineral forms giant six-sided crystals. A crystal that was 60 pounds (27 kilograms) and two feet (61 centimeters) long was cut into the world's largest aquamarine gem—the Dom Pedro aquamarine. Other types of beryl have formed the largest crystals of any mineral ever found. One from Madagascar weighs a mighty 380 tons and measures 60 feet (18 meters) long.

This mineral was popular as a gemstone among sailors and travelers. They believed it prevented them from getting seasick or becoming shipwrecked.

 A thousand years ago, people with poor eyesight might use a magnifying glass or reading stone made of beryl. At the time, glass was too blurry to use.

 Beryl can be a source of the very rare metal beryllium. The metal is so light and tough that it was used to coat the mirrors of the James Webb Space Telescope.

Fact file

Substance: Mineral
Type: Silicate
Found: Pegmatites, hydrothermal veins
Hot spots: Brazil, Tanzania, Mozambique, Nigeria, Madagascar, Pakistan
Typical colors: Pale blue to light green
Properties: 7.5–8 hardness

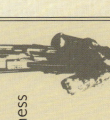

Sandstone

Sedimentary rock

- Sandstone is a type of sedimentary rock. Sedimentary rocks are made from grains or sediments that piled up on the seafloor, in rivers, or in deserts long ago. The grains were buried, then squeezed and cemented together over millions of years until they turned into tough rock.

- Some sedimentary rocks stay buried forever, but many are lifted to the surface by the movement of the Earth. They can be seen in thick layers called strata. These layers sometimes remain flat, but many are crumpled up due to pressure from deep underground.

- Sandstone is made from sand—little grains left behind from other rocks as they were attacked by the weather. Sandstones are mostly made of quartz grains but can contain feldspar, calcite, clay, and mica.

- A kind of sandstone called Old Red Sandstone is made from the sand of vast deserts that covered Europe 400 million years ago.

Fact file

Substance: Rock
Type: Sedimentary
Found: Deserts, riverbeds, coastal areas
Hot spots: Scotland, Italy, USA
Typical color: Sandy
Properties: Sand grains

The buttes and mesas, or towers and plateaus, of the Arizona deserts are made of tough sandstone. Over time, streams, wind, and ice ate the softer surrounding rock away, leaving incredible sandstone shapes jutting up from the flat desert floor.

 When wet sandstone is soft enough, it can be sliced to make blocks for building houses. The White House in Washington, DC, is made from old gray sandstone that has been painted white.

Jade

Sodium aluminum silicate

- Jade is a kind of metamorphic mineral called a pyroxene. It forms when rocks are buried deep in the Earth at high pressures but stay quite cold. Jade comes in two varieties—jadeite and nephrite. Jadeite is harder, shinier, and rarer than nephrite.

- This mineral is very hard and glassy and usually green or white. It can be polished to a high shine. In the Stone Age, it was often used to make axes and knives.

- When the Spanish invaded Central America in the 1500s, the local people told them jade cured kidney problems. So the Spanish called the stone *piedra de ijada*, or "stone of the side," giving us the name jade in English.

- The Chinese have been carving jade to make statues and jewelry for thousands of years. They carved jade into dragons, lions, and dogs as well as religious figures such as the Buddha. They mostly used nephrite from Khotan and Yarkand in Xinjiang.

Fact file

Substance: Mineral

Type: Silicate

Found: In metamorphosed rock

Hot spots: Russia, Myanmar, Guatemala, China

Typical colors: Green, white

Properties: 6.5–7 hardness

The Aztecs, Maya, and other Mesoamericans carved jadeite into figurines, amulets, and small masks in various shades of green. All Mesoamerican jade came from Guatemala.

 Jade is very difficult to carve but can remain in good condition for a long time. Because jade was thought to last forever, rulers in ancient China were sometimes buried in suits made from jade plates sewn together with gold thread.

Galena

Lead sulfide

- Galena often forms shiny, chunky crystals that look like a pile of metal cubes. It typically forms in hydrothermal veins—cracks full of hot volcanic fluid.

- Galena contains a large amount of the metal lead. It can often be more than 80 percent lead and is the main ore for that metal. Ores are minerals and rocks that we get metals from.

- Galena is sometimes called lead glance. Glance comes from the German word *glanz*, which translates as shine, due to the quality of galena's shiny crystals.

- This mineral was used for its lead in ancient times. Because lead melts at a low temperature, it could be melted out of galena over just an ordinary wood fire, making it an easy metal to access.

Fact file

Substance: Mineral

Type: Sulfide

Found: Hydrothermal veins, limestone beds

Hot spots: Australia, Germany, England, Sardinia

Typical color: Dark gray

Properties: 2.5 hardness

Lead is simple to mold and does not corrode, or waste away. It was used to make water pipes in Roman times. For centuries, most water pipes were made from lead until people realized the metal is poisonous.

 Galena, Illinois, is one of many towns so named because of local lead mines.

35

Marble

Metamorphic rock

- Marble is a metamorphic rock. It was originally limestone that was crushed under mountains as Earth's surface moved and then was cooked by the heat and pressure. These forces transformed the dull gray limestone into shiny white marble.

- The mineral calcite is what makes marble white. Sometimes impurities can give the rock swirling, colored ripples or even stain parts of the marble a different color. Pyroxene makes marble green, graphite turns it black, and sphene colors it yellow.

- Marble was used to cover India's Taj Mahal, one of the world's most famous buildings. This huge structure looks like an ornate palace, but in fact the Emperor Shah Jahan had it built as a tomb for his wife, Mumtaz Mahal.

- Powdered marble is sometimes used in toothpaste to provide a gentle grit to help clean teeth.

Fact file

Substance: Rock
Type: Metamorphic
Found: Mountain regions
Hot spots: Italy, Spain, China, India, Greece
Typical colors: White, streaky
Properties: 3–5 hardness

◆ This rock is perfect for carving into sculptures. This is because it is not too hard and keeps its shape for a long time—some marble sculptures are more than 2,500 years old. The famous Italian artist Michelangelo carved his huge, 17-foot (five-meter) statue of David from a single block of white marble.

◆ The most famous marble of all comes from the Carrara quarry in northern Italy. The marble there is often pure white and is ideal for sculpting. It has been quarried since Roman times, when it was called moon marble.

Hematite

Iron oxide

- Hematite is a hard and heavy mineral. It gets its name from the ancient Greek word for blood because of the red color of some types of hematite.

- The mineral is made from at least two-thirds iron and is the world's main ore, or source rock, of iron. It is the iron rusting that can make it red.

- Hematite forms in many ways, typically when other iron-rich minerals such as magnetite and siderite get altered by water and the weather.

- When hematite forms in knobbly lumps that look a little like kidneys, it is called kidney ore. It can also form in steel-gray, needlelike crystals called specular hematite.

Fact file

Substance: Mineral

Type: Oxide

Found: Sedimentary rocks

Hot spots: Australia, USA, Brazil, Venezuela

Typical colors: Red, brown, black, gray

Properties: 5.5–6.5 hardness

A lot of the world's hematite comes from quarries near Lake Superior on the United States border with Canada.

 Hematite ore, along with some magnetite, provided iron for the world's first all-iron bridge, built in 1779 in Shropshire, England.

Unakite

Metamorphic rock

- This rock was originally granite but was altered by extreme heat and pressure under Earth's surface in a process called metamorphism.

- Unakite has a mottled mix of colors. The pale gray patches are quartz, while the green comes from the mineral epidote. The pink is from the mineral orthoclase feldspar. The epidote was also originally orthoclase feldspar but has metamorphosed, or changed.

- The rock is often found as pebbles in the material carried by glaciers or washed down in rivers from mountains. The pebbles can be polished into semiprecious stones.

- Its unusual combination of colors makes unakite a popular decorative stone. It is used for making jewelry, such as beads, and for animal carvings, eggs, and spheres.

Fact file

Substance: Rock
Type: Metamorphic
Found: Pebbles, cobbles
Hot spots: USA, South Africa, Sierra Leone
Typical colors: Green and pink
Properties: Medium grain size

Unakite gets its name from the Unaka mountain range in North Carolina, where it was first identified in 1874. It has since been found in many other places around the world.

Gold

Native gold

- Gold is one of the few native elements. An element is a natural substance that cannot be broken down into another one. This means gold can be found in the ground as a pure metal, just like copper and silver. Other metals are mixed in with rock. They have to be melted to get them out by making the rock very hot.

- Pure gold never corrodes, or breaks down, and stays bright and shiny almost forever. When the tomb of the Egyptian boy king Tutankhamun was discovered in 1922, his solid gold burial mask gleamed like it did when he was buried more than 3,000 years before.

- This mineral usually forms in veins alongside gray or colorless quartz. Veins are created when hot, salty water moves through rocks. Gold is released from the hot liquid as it cools down.

- When rocks with gold veins inside are worn down by the weather over millions of years, small gold grains are washed into rivers. Prospectors, or gold hunters, can find these grains by carefully swilling and sifting river sand in a pan. The gold is heavy, so it stays in the pan while the lighter sand drains away.

Fact file

Substance: Metal

Type: Native element

Found: Veins in volcanic rock, river sand

Hot spots: South Africa, USA, Indonesia, Australia, Canada

Typical color: Gold

Properties: 2.5–3 hardness

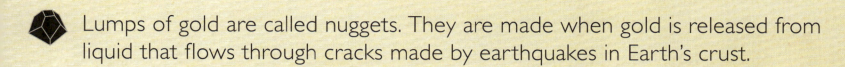 Lumps of gold are called nuggets. They are made when gold is released from liquid that flows through cracks made by earthquakes in Earth's crust.

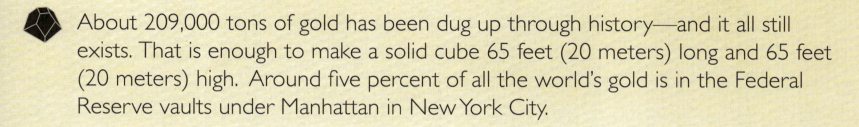 About 209,000 tons of gold has been dug up through history—and it all still exists. That is enough to make a solid cube 65 feet (20 meters) long and 65 feet (20 meters) high. Around five percent of all the world's gold is in the Federal Reserve vaults under Manhattan in New York City.

Turquoise

Copper aluminum phosphate

- ◆ Turquoise is known for its distinctive bright blue-green color, which has given its name to the color turquoise.

- ◆ Turquoise forms in hot, dry places where small amounts of water seep into rocks rich in copper and aluminum. It is the copper that gives the stone its blue color. The more copper, the bluer the stone.

- ◆ It might look like plain stone, but under a microscope, turquoise has tiny crystals. This is why it is desribed as being cryptocrystalline—crypto means hidden.

- ◆ Turquoise got its name because in the 1600s, many of the best stones in Europe came through Turkey from mines in Persia. Turquoise means Turkish stone.

Fact file

Substance: Mineral
Type: Phosphate
Found: Deserts
Hot spots: Southwest USA; Iran; Sinai, Egypt
Typical color: Blue-green
Properties: 5–6 hardness

Some Native Americans believed the blue in turquoise symbolized the sky and the green the earth. They told how it fell from the sky and called it fallen sky stone.

 The name of one of the most important Aztec gods, Xiuhtecuhtli, came from the Nahuatl word for turquoise. The word also meant year, so Xiuhtecuhtli represented time as well as turquoise. He is often shown with a crown and objects made of turquoise.

Gypsum

Calcium sulfate dihydrate

- Gypsum is one of the most common minerals found on Earth's surface. It is a powdery stone left behind when salty water evaporates. It typically forms in places where there were once salty lagoons and shallow seas.

- Gypsum is typically soft and powdery. It is the main ingredient in plaster, which is used to make the walls and ceiling of homes smooth.

- Under particular conditions, gypsum can sometimes form long, thin, silky crystals called satin spar. It can also form chunky crystals called selenite. The giant crystals in Mexico's Cueva de los Cristales, or Cave of the Crystals, are selenite.

- A white stone called alabaster is a type of gypsum that looks very like marble. It is much softer than marble and has been used for carving into sculptures since ancient times.

Fact file

Substance: Mineral

Type: Sulfate

Found: Dried-up salty lagoons and shallow seas

Hot spots: China, USA, Brazil, Iran, Spain, Mexico

Typical color: White

Properties: 2 hardness

We eat lots of gypsum. That is because food makers use it to bulk up ice cream, spaghetti, bread, cereal, pills, and even tofu.

 White Sands National Park in New Mexico has giant sand dunes of pure gypsum. They are made from tiny gypsum crystals.

Basalt

Extrusive igneous rock

- Basalt is a black volcanic rock. It is created when superhot magma from beneath Earth's crust floods up through volcanoes onto the surface and then freezes solid.

- Basalt lava often comes up through cracks in the ocean floor. As it hits cold water and quickly cools, it freezes to the ocean bed around the crack to form new seafloor, widening the ocean as it does.

- Rocks such as basalt form from lava that erupts aboveground before turning solid. These are called extrusive igneous or volcanic rocks. Intrusive igneous rocks are made from magma that becomes solid underground. We call molten rock magma when it is underground and lava when it reaches the surface.

- The lava that forms basalt is superhot. This is because it mostly erupts where Earth's crust is thinnest, particularly under the ocean. Here, the magma has little time to cool as it rises.

Fact file

Substance: Rock
Type: Extrusive igneous
Found: Ocean floor, vast plateaus
Hot spots: Columbia River Plateau, USA; Deccan Traps, India
Typical color: Black
Properties: Fine grains

- All rocks are made from tiny particles called grains or from the crystals of minerals. Basalt's grains are very fine, or small.

- Northern Ireland's Giant's Causeway is known for its natural rock columns. They cracked into pillars as basalt lava cooled millions of years ago.

- The darker patches on the Moon's surface known as seas are really plateaus formed from floods of basalt lava. They were made early in the Moon's life.

Amber

Fossilized resin

- Amber is the fossilized resin of ancient trees. Long ago, trees needing to protect themselves from disease and insects produced a sticky liquid called resin. The resin oozed down the trunk and hardened into lumpy drops. Over time, it fossilized into a substance that can be polished to make the soft stone amber.

- Some insects and other creatures were trapped and preserved inside amber as resin turned hard. People have discovered 99 million-year-old ants, 25 million-year-old scorpions, Caribbean lizards, and even meat-eating plants imprisoned in amber.

- The most famous amber is found in sands around the Baltic Sea, especially on the Samland Peninsular near Kaliningrad in Russia. It formed some 40 million years ago.

- Natural materials that look like minerals but do not have the crystals of a mineral, or that are made by living things, are called mineraloids. Amber, pearl, and jet are all mineraloids.

Fact file

Substance: Mineraloid
Type: Fossilized resin
Found: Hard drops found in sand
Hot spots: Baltic
Typical colors: Amber, honey
Properties: 2–2.5 hardness

◆ Dinosaur feathers have been found trapped in amber. Mosquitos preserved in amber might have sucked on dinosaur blood, so scientists once thought they could get the DNA from this blood and re-create dinosaurs, just like in the movie *Jurassic Park*. But they discovered that the DNA has not survived.

◆ Amber is one of the birthstones for November. Some people believe it represents courage.

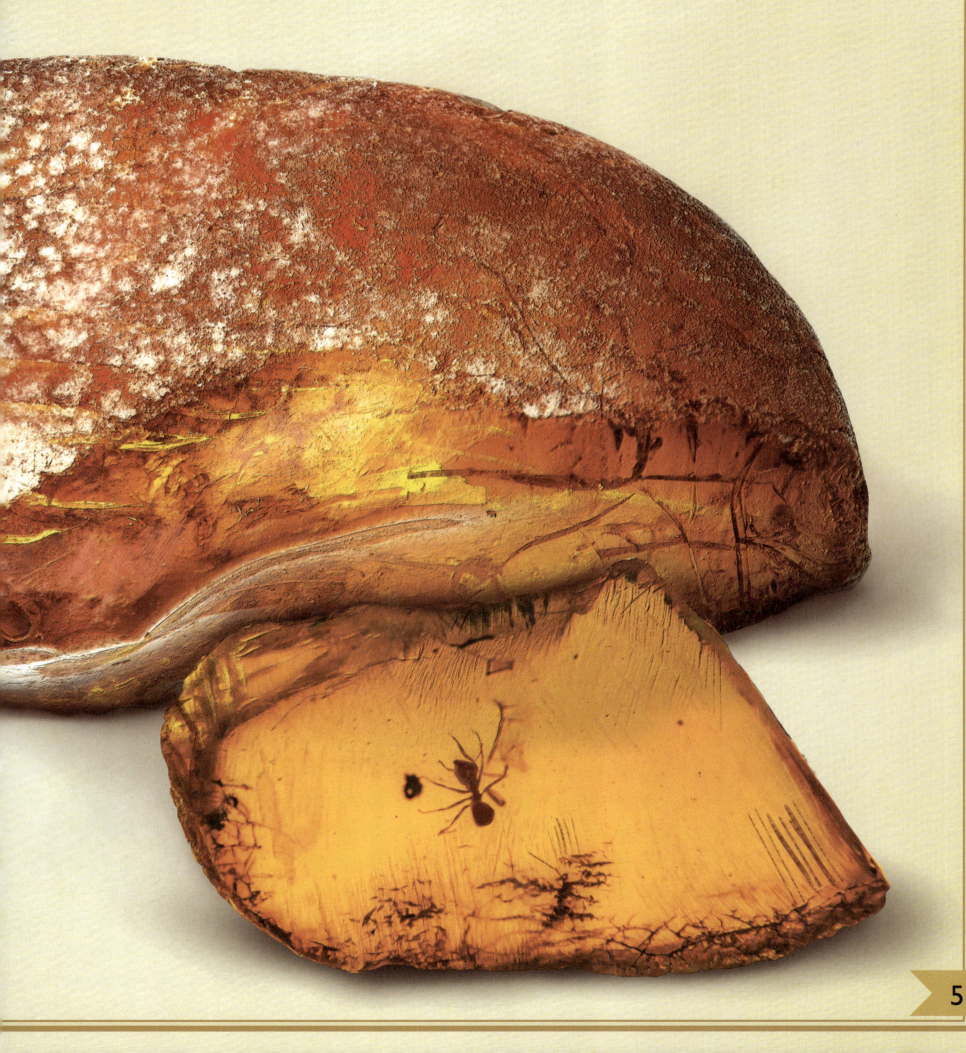

Calcite

Calcium carbonate

- Calcite is a whitish mineral that makes up most of the world's limestone rocks. It is also what bones, teeth, and seashells are made of.

- The calcite in limestone came mostly from the bones and shells of sea creatures that were buried and crushed long ago to make the rock.

- Iceland spar is a type of pure calcite that forms in these clear, icelike blocks. It was so called because it was discovered in Iceland and was common there. Spar means a crystal with a smooth surface. Iceland spar is known for showing a double image when the crystal is looked through.

- Viking sailors might have used Iceland spar calcite crystals to help them find the Sun and navigate even when it was cloudy. This is because the crystals polarize light—that is, they separate light from different directions, allowing the sailors to locate the Sun through the clouds.

Fact file

Substance: Mineral
Type: Carbonate
Found: Limestone, shells, bones
Hot spots: Iceland
Typical color: White
Properties: 3 hardness

Strange, otherworldly formations hanging from cave ceilings and jutting from their floors are mostly calcite. They are made from the slow buildup of minerals dissolved in dripping water. Stalactites hang down and stalagmites poke up.

 There are 500 trillion tons of calcite dissolved in the oceans. Shellfish take this calcite from the seawater to build their shells.

Granite

Intrusive igneous rock

- Granite is an intrusive igneous rock. Igneous rocks are formed from magma, or liquid rock, from Earth's superhot interior. As magma comes nearer to the surface, it cools and turns into solid rock. Igneous rock is called intrusive when it becomes solid underground without ever reaching Earth's surface.

- The rock is speckled because it is made of three minerals—quartz, feldspar, and mica. The speckles are their small crystals or grains. Granite's grains are mostly big enough to see. This is because the magma it formed from cooled slowly underground, giving time for the grains to grow.

- This rock is very tough. We often see areas of granite exposed aboveground when softer rock on top is worn away by the weather over time.

- One of the most famous monuments in the United States, Mount Rushmore, is carved from a granite rock face. It depicts four of the country's greatest presidents.

Fact file

Substance: Rock

Type: Intrusive igneous

Found: Mountain regions

Hot spots: Sierra Nevada, USA; England; Scandinavia

Typical colors: Speckled gray, pink

Properties: Coarse grains

Granite has many modern uses. It can be polished into hard, sparkly surfaces for kitchens and buildings or used for floors. In ancient times, granite was used for the pharaoh's sarcophagus in the Great Pyramid of Giza.

 The famous and imposing rock formation known as Half Dome in California's Yosemite National Park is part of a huge batholith made of granodiorite, a rock similar to granite. Batholiths are giant underground lumps of rock. It was pushed up from under Earth's surface and shaped by ancient glaciers.

Topaz

Aluminum fluohydroxisilicate

- Topaz is one of the hardest of all gems, after diamond. It forms in cracks and veins in granite and in mineral-rich bands of igneous rock called pegmatites. Topaz is found in mountains, especially in Brazil.

- The word *topaz* is said to come from the ancient name for Zabargad Island in the Red Sea in Egypt, where the stones were thought to originate. Many topazes in ancient times actually came from Sri Lanka.

- It is possible to go hunting for topaz on Topaz Mountain in Utah. Its presence there helped it become the state gemstone of Utah.

- Until 200 years ago, jewelers called all yellow gemstones topaz. It was later realized that topaz is a specific type of mineral and that other gems can be yellow, too. Topaz can also come in different colors.

Fact file

Substance: Mineral
Type: Silicate
Found: Granite pegmatites
Hot spots: Brazil, South Asia, USA, Russia
Typical colors: Yellow, blue
Properties: 8 hardness

Orange topaz is the most precious kind of topaz because of its rarity and striking color. It is a birthstone for November.

 The ancient Romans believed topaz protected travelers from harm. In India, it was said that topaz brought beauty, intelligence, and long life if worn next to the heart.

Copper

Native copper

- Like gold, copper is a native element. That means you can find pure copper in the ground. This is why it was probably the first metal humans ever used, perhaps more than 10,000 years ago, for coins and ornaments.

- Copper is typically found near volcanoes, in veins running through the rock where hot liquids once flowed. Rocks rich in copper veins are called porphyry coppers.

- Unlike gold, copper changes when in contact with air, acquiring a green coating called verdigris. That is why it is rare to see the metal as copper-colored in the ground.

- About 5,000 years ago, people started to mix a little tin with copper to make a tough metal called bronze. This began the Bronze Age. The first ever swords, shields, and helmets were made of bronze.

Fact file

Substance: Metal
Type: Native element
Found: Veins in volcanic rock
Hot spots: Chile, Peru, China, DRC, USA
Typical colors: Copper, pale green
Properties: 2.5–3 hardness

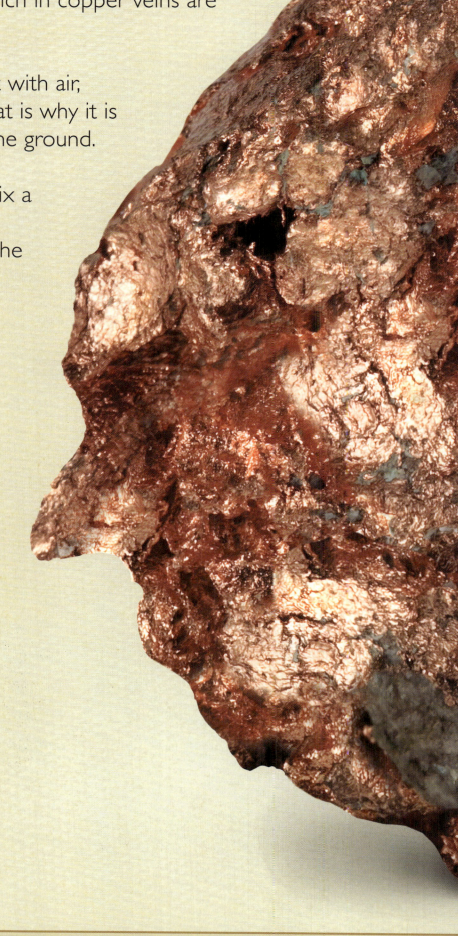

◆ Because it is rare to find pure copper in the ground, today we mostly get copper from ore minerals. These are rocks that contain copper, which has to be melted out. Most of the world's copper comes from mines in Chile, Peru, China, the Democratic Republic of the Congo, and the United States.

◆ Copper allows electricity to flow through it very easily, so most electrical wires are made of copper.

Halite

Sodium chloride

- Halite is the mineral or crystal form of salt—it is made of the same chemicals as the salt we put in food. It occurs naturally as a rock, which is why it is also called rock salt.

- Some halite formed where seawater evaporated long ago, leaving behind vast beds of rock salt. These beds can be buried over time, so rock salt must often be mined.

- Some of the world's oldest salt mines are at Xiechi Lake in China. They are thought to be thousands of years old.

- The Wieliczka salt mine in Poland has been dug since the 1200s. It is so vast that miners and artists carved underground chapels out of the salt!

- In the past, halite from salt mines provided most of our salt, which was used mainly for food. Now a lot of salt comes from evaporating seawater.

Fact file

Substance: Mineral

Type: Salt

Found: Evaporated salt lagoons

Hot spots: China, Russia, Bolivia, Dead Sea

Typical colors: White, pink, blue

Properties: 2 hardness

Most of the salt mined or from seawater is used to make chemicals or manufactured products, such as soap, baking soda, and plastics. Only a small amount is made to be used with food.

 Rock salt is usually colorless or white but can also be brown, pink, or blue depending on other materials contained in it.

Cinnabar

Mercury sulfide

- This strikingly colored red mineral forms near Earth's surface from hot fluid in hydrothermal veins—cracks near volcanoes. It also forms around hot springs.

- Cinnabar is the main ore, or source stone, of mercury. Mercury is the only metal that is liquid at room temperature.

- In Roman times, cinnabar was often confused with the red sap that oozes from a tree, now given the scientific name *Dracaena cinnabari*. The tree grows on the island of Socotra in the Arabian Sea, and its sap is known as dragon's blood.

- In the past, when artists wanted bright red, they used vermilion paint, which was made from cinnabar.

- Cinnabar was used in traditional medicine to give people energy. People later realized the mercury in it actually makes it poisonous, so it may have done more harm than good.

Fact file

Substance: Mineral
Type: Sulfide
Found: Shallow veins, hot springs
Hot spots: Spain, Slovenia
Typical colors: Shades of red
Properties: 2–2.5 hardness

For thousands of years, cinnabar was ground into powder and used to color things, from paints and inks to dyes and even makeup. The red in many ancient cave paintings, such as at Lascaux in France, is made from cinnabar. The ancient Romans also used the red of cinnabar on the walls of their homes.

Peridotite

Intrusive igneous rock

- Peridotite is the most common rock on Earth. Most of it is hidden deep down beneath our feet, inside Earth's hot, rocky mantle.

- Unusually, peridotite is a green rock. That is because it contains the green mineral olivine.

- Dunite is a form of peridotite. It also contains chromite and is the world's main source of supershiny chromium. Chromium is used to coat everything from kettles to car bumpers in mirrorlike chrome.

- Peridotite has its own gemstone, peridot, which is made from pure olivine. Peridot is actually mostly taken from basalt rock. It is the only gem that ever comes in just a single color—deep green.

Fact file

Substance: Rock
Type: Intrusive igneous
Found: Earth's mantle
Hot spots: England, USA, New Zealand
Typical color: Dark green
Properties: Medium to coarse grains

This rock occasionally oozes up from the mantle. By the time it reaches Earth's surface, it is usually completely changed, having melted to form basalt magma.

 In a few places, superhot peridotite magma drives up to the surface from the depths through narrow volcanic pipes. These pipes are called kimberlites and are named after the famous Kimberley diamond mine in South Africa. They can bring with them ancient diamonds, forged deep down billions of years ago.

Limestone

Biochemical sedimentary rock

- Limestone is mostly made from the bones and shells of countless creatures that lived in the sea long ago. Their remains settled on the seafloor and over time were buried, squeezed, and cemented together to form hard rock.

- Most of the limestone we see today formed over hundreds of thousands of years, but new rock is forming in places around the world even today.

- The fossils of ancient sea creatures can often be seen preserved in limestone rock like the one pictured here. These can tell scientists what life and environments were like millions of years ago.

- Limestone is typically made from giant blocks created when the rock dried out and cracked as it was forming. On the top surface, these blocks can look like paving stones. The cracks allow water to seep through the rock.

Fact file

Substance: Rock
Type: Biochemical sediment
Found: Thick layers in the ground
Hot spots: Australia, Slovenia, China
Typical color: Pale gray
Properties: Fine grains

Rainwater is slightly acidic and can erode, or eat away, at limestone as it seeps into cracks. Eroded cracks can create a weird landscape of pillars, gorges, and caverns called karst. Most cave systems are found in areas of limestone.

 Limestone is a very popular building material. It has been used throughout history for buildings ranging from the Great Pyramid of Giza in Egypt to Buckingham Palace in the United Kingdom.

Diamond

Carbon

- Diamond is incredibly tough, shiny, and extremely old. Most natural diamonds formed under massive heat and pressure deep down in the Earth at least a billion years ago. Some are even older.

- In a few places, superhot magma from deep inside the Earth powers to the surface in natural pipes called kimberlites before hardening. As the magma spews from below, it can drag diamonds to the surface.

- Along with sulfur, diamond is the only nonmetal element found naturally in the ground. Diamond is made from pure carbon. It is the hardest natural material on Earth, which is why it is used on drill bits to cut through glass or even rock.

- The Cullinan Diamond, dug up in South Africa, was the largest diamond ever found and made into a gem. It weighed one pound, six ounces (621 grams) and was cut into many precious stones, which were used in the Crown Jewels of the United Kingdom's royal family.

Fact file

Substance: Mineral
Type: High-pressure carbon
Found: Kimberlite pipes
Hot spots: Russia, Botswana, Angola, South Africa, Canada
Typical color: Colorless
Properties: 10 hardness

Astronomers have found a distant planet that might be made entirely of carbon, a third of which could be diamond. They think they have also discovered a dying star that is changing into pure, solid diamond as it cools, shrinks, and turns into crystals—although this process will take billions of years.

Tourmaline

Sodium lithium aluminum silicon oxide

- Tourmaline is the most colorful mineral group of all. Tourmaline crystals come in a kaleidoscope of colors, and even a single crystal can be multicolored!

- The most spectacular tourmaline crystals are from places with hydrothermal activity—areas with naturally hot underground water, such as hot springs and geysers. The hot waters and vapors carry minerals into pockets, gaps, and fractures in the rocks. As the minerals settle and cool over time, crystals begin to grow.

- Tourmaline is not just one mineral but a mix of related minerals. Each type of tourmaline contains its own blend of chemicals, with each one producing a different color stone.

- If conditions change as tourmaline crystals grow, the crystals can form bands of different colors. These are called zoned crystals. This watermelon tourmaline has a zone of green around a pink center, just like a watermelon.

Fact file

Substance: Mineral

Type: Silicate

Found: With igneous and metamorphic rocks

Hot spots: Brazil, USA, Nigeria, Mozambique

Typical colors: 100 combinations

Properties: 7–7.5 hardness

The ancient Egyptians called tourmaline rainbow rock. They believed it soaked up all its colors as it passed through a rainbow on its journey from the center of the Earth.

 The most sought-after tourmaline is paraiba. Paraiba tourmaline gets its electric-blue color from traces of copper. A crystal with a little manganese in it gives tourmaline a slight purple tint.

Obsidian

Glassy volcanic rock

- Obsidian is a black volcanic glass. Volcanic glasses are made from lava that loses its water and cools so quickly that no crystals can form.

- This rock is much tougher than the glass used in buildings, but when hit with a hammer, it also shatters into very sharp fragments. Obsidian fragments have sharp, curved edges like blades rather than the splintered edges of normal glass.

- In the Stone Age, obsidian was highly prized because it could be fractured to make very sharp knives and arrowheads. These took time, practice, and great skill to make.

- Sometimes obsidian comes in rainbow colors, gold, or green. Mahogany obsidian is brown with black streaks, like the wood it is named after. Midnight lace obsidian got its contorted stripes as lava slowly rolled and stretched as it cooled.

Fact file

Substance: Rock
Type: Volcanic
Found: Rapidly cooled lava flows
Hot spots: USA, Scotland, Iceland
Typical colors: Black, brown
Properties: No grains

◆ The ancient Aztecs viewed obsidian as sacred. They used it for a famous mask representing Tezcatlipoca, the god of the night sky, now kept in the British Museum in London.

◆ Most obsidian outcrops are small, but there are huge formations in Valles Caldera in New Mexico and at Glass Buttes in Oregon.

Amethyst

Silicon dioxide

- Amethyst is a type of quartz, a hard mineral made of silicon dioxide. Quartz is one of the most common minerals in Earth's crust. This, along with quartz's toughness, means grains of quartz are what is mostly left behind when rocks are broken down over time—that is why sand is mostly quartz.

- This mineral is known for its chunky purple crystals. The purple color comes from the presence of iron. Fluorite is just about the only other mineral that can have the same deep purple. This makes amethyst easy to recognize.

- When amethyst is heated, its stones can turn yellow.

- Sometimes amethyst crystals form inside geodes, or bubblelike spaces in the rock. Geodes look like dull, gray, round stones on the outside, but when they are cracked open, a glittering array of crystals is revealed. The largest amethyst geodes are found in Brazil and Uruguay.

- Amethyst is just one of many kinds of quartz. Others are stripy tiger's eye, yellow citrine, and chalcedony, which looks a bit like a hard candy.

Fact file

Substance: Mineral

Type: Silicate

Found: Small holes in volcanic rock

Hot spots: Brazil, Uruguay, Sri Lanka, Madagascar

Typical colors: Shades of purple

Properties: 7 hardness

An old story tells how amethyst got its color from the nymph Amethystos. The tale goes that she was turned to stone by the ancient Greek goddess Artemis to save her from the tigers of Dionysus, the god of wine. Dionysus was full of regret and poured red wine over the statue, turning the white stone to purple amethyst.

Malachite

Copper carbonate hydroxide

- Malachite is a green, stripy mineral that forms when copper-rich rock is exposed to the air.

- This mineral often forms in round lumps in cavities where copper-rich water drips through the rocks. These lumps can be sliced to reveal malachite's curved rings.

- The green sheen sometimes seen on copper and bronze, known as verdigris, is a kind of malachite.

- Malachite from Russia's Ural Mountains was highly prized by Russian emperors. They used it to decorate a room in their Winter Palace in St. Petersburg with pillars, a fireplace, and an urn carved from malachite.

Fact file

Substance: Mineral
Type: Carbonate
Found: Underground cavities
Hot spots: Ural Mountains, Russia
Typical color: Green
Properties: 3.5–4 hardness

Vivid green malachite is a signpost to copper deposits in the rock. Sometimes an excess of water can turn green malachite into blue azurite minerals.

 The ancient Egyptians used malachite for its bright green color in tomb painting. This was because for them, the color green represented life, death, growth, and resurrection. They also used malachite for eye makeup and carved it into jewelry and ornaments.

Garnet

Calcium iron silicate

- Garnets are gemstones that come in various colors, but the best known is red. They have been traded for centuries for use as a gem but also for their hardness and ability to grind down softer gems.

- These stones form deep underground in metamorphic rock, such as schist, as minerals in the rock are altered by extreme heat and pressure. Garnets are sometimes found decorating the schist rocks like cherries in a cake.

- Garnets are mined from rocks that have been lifted nearer the surface. They are also often found washed into streams after the rock containing them was worn away by wind, rain, and ice.

- There are 20 kinds of garnet, but only five are used as gems. These are pyrope, almandine, spessartine, grossular, and andradite.

Fact file

Substance: Mineral

Type: Silicate

Found: Metamorphic rocks and streams

Hot spots: India, Brazil, Namibia, Tanzania, Madagascar

Typical colors: Red, green, gray

Properties: 6.5–7.5 hardness

Demantoid is a rich green form of garnet that sparkles as brightly as diamond. Blue is the rarest color of garnet. Pyrope–spessartine garnet changes color from blue-green to purple depending on the light it is viewed in.

 In ancient stories, Noah's ark used a lantern made of garnet as its only source of light to show the way in the dark.

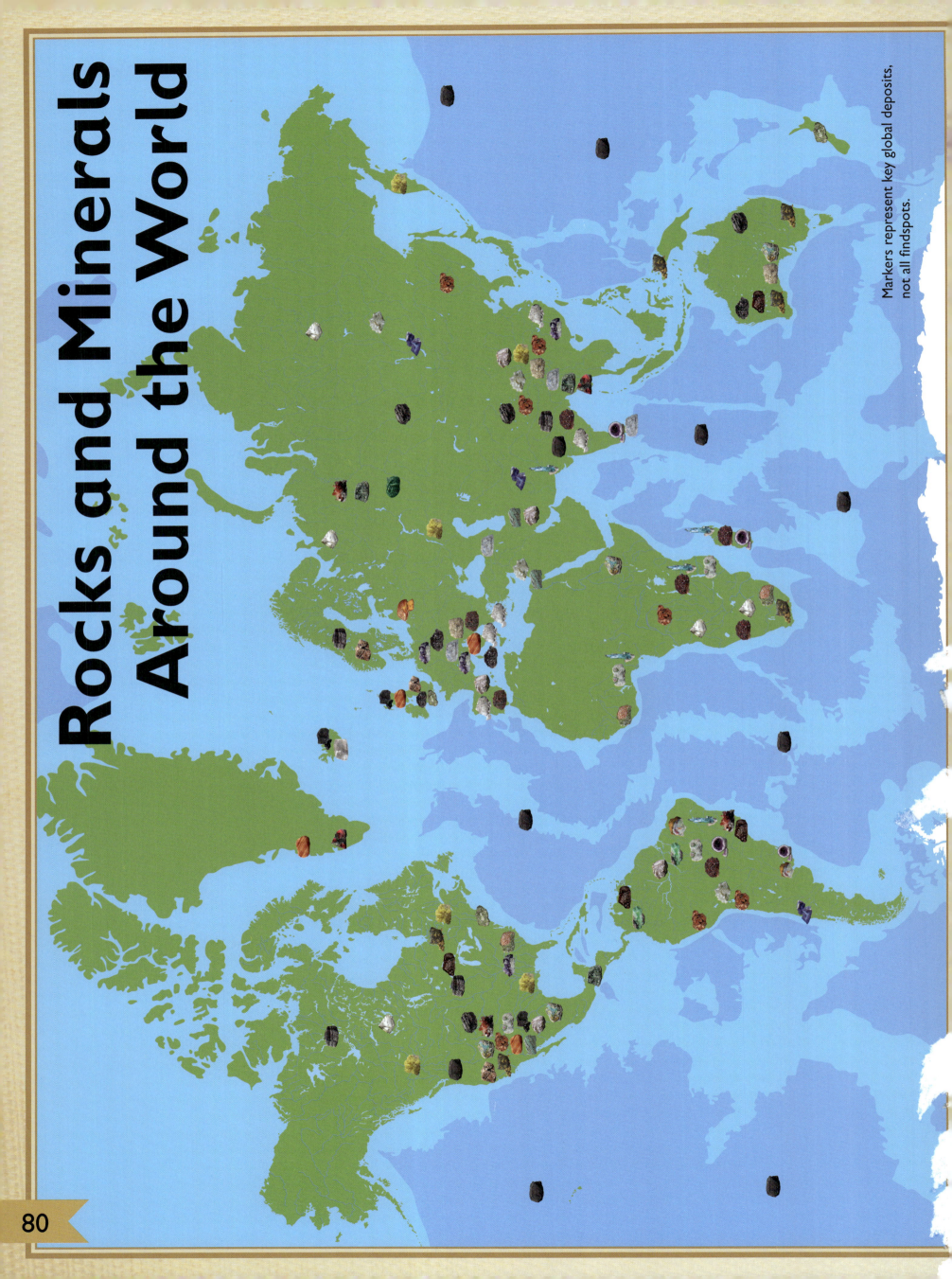

Rocks and Minerals Around the World

Markers represent key global deposits, not all findspots.

80